After the Pain

You Can Start Over

Sharon Ewell

After The Pain: You Can Start Over
Copyright © August 11, 2021
Sharon Ewell
ISBN# 978-1-953526-13-7

All rights reserved under international copyright law. This book or parts thereof may not be reproduced in any form, stored in a retrieval system, or transmitted in any form by any means; electronic, mechanical, photocopy, recording, or otherwise without prior written permission of the publisher or author, except as provided by United States of America copyright.

Published by TaylorMade Publishing
Jacksonville, FL
www.TaylorMadePublishingFL.com
(904) 323-1334

Table of Contents

Dedication i
Chapter 1 - In the Beginning.. 1
Chapter 2 – The Transfer 4
Chapter 3 – The Delivery 6
Chapter 4 - Teen Mom Life 8
Chapter 5 - Unexpected Visitor 9
Chapter 6 - Tired, Tired... 10
Chapter 7 - Marriage... 13
Chapter 8 - Fights, More Babies & Cheating 15
Chapter 9 - Separation 19
Chapter 10 - Pimping... 21
Chapter 11 - Hell Breaks Loose.................................. 22
Chapter 12 - Life Change 25
Chapter 13 - Pain in the Process................................ 26
Chapter 14 - After the Pain.. 29
Chapter 15 - After the Pain, You Can Start Over 31
More Pain – A Shattered Heart 32
"That Smile" 33
"The Side Effects of You" 35
"I Got Lost".. 38
"I Heard My Daddy Saying to Me" 41
"My Fault".. 43
About the Author 45

Dedication

I dedicate this book to my daddy and mama and my brother and sister. I hope I've made you all proud. I miss you all terribly. I take you all with me everywhere I go because y'all are right here in my heart.

God took this book in a totally different direction than what I expected, and I followed just what He wanted me to write in it. You can't go wrong when you are obedient to God.

Chapter 1 - In the Beginning

It all started when I turned 15 years old. I was a rebellious child, all because I felt like my mama loved her sons and her niece more than me, her one and only daughter. Aren't a mother and daughter supposed to have an unbreakable bond?

Well, that didn't exist in my world. Maybe it was because I felt like some attention from my mama was better than no attention. Yes, I did things I knew I shouldn't do. I'll admit that I deliberately did crazy things so I could get some attention from her. Now, don't get me wrong, I'm not blaming my mama for me doing the things I did, because that was strictly my choice. I rebelled against just about everything she told me. The boys could get away with anything, but me, on the other hand, not so much. This was not fair at all. I fought all the time and stayed suspended from school.

I had to go before the Board of Education a total of four times. Every time I went, there was this little old lady taking notes, looking at me over her glasses and shaking her head at me. I would think to myself, 'What is this old butt lady looking at and why the heck is she shaking her head at me?' However, I dared not say anything with my mama sitting next to me. I knew better. You see, in those days, it was okay for our parents to lay hands on us; and my mama would've hit me in my mouth and closed it. So, I quietly sat there and talked crazy to that old lady in my head.

Needless to say, the Board was sick of seeing me there and had been threatening to kick me out of all Kansas City public schools because of my behavior. But they kept giving me chance after chance because of my grades. Yeah, I made good grades when I was in school. But this time was different. They decided to send me to an alternative school for troubled kids. Humboldt was the name of the school.

Pregnant teenagers had classes on the top floors of the school, and the bad kids' classes were on the bottom floors. Long story short, word got back to the principal that I was pregnant, and he called me to his office.

I went in there and sat down and he asked me if I was pregnant. I looked away, hung my head, and nodded, 'yes.'

He said to me, "Shay, look at me." So, I did.

He asked me again, "Are you pregnant?"

With an attitude, I said, "Yes."

He said, "Okay, I will be transferring you upstairs to the teen pregnancy school."

I was like, whatever. Do what you feel you got to do. I really don't care.

So, then, he started preaching to me about me being pregnant and my bad attitude.

I got up and told him, "I'm not trying to hear anything."

I stormed out, slamming the door behind me. He came after me, but I refused to stop because I didn't want to hear his mouth. He yelled, "Miss Henderson, you're asking for trouble and for what? I am just trying to help you." I kept right on walking. I went back to class and finished my work.

At the end of the school day, I was on my way to the school bus to go home. I went outside and there was a big fight going on, so the guards escorted us to our buses. I was trying to watch the fight but was made to get on the bus. I wanted to get home so I could eat. The baby growing inside me kept me starving. I told my mama they were transferring me to the teen pregnancy school upstairs.

She said, "Okay, and why didn't they let me know?"

I just shrugged my shoulders and went to bed.

Chapter 2 – The Transfer

I woke up and got ready for my first day of being in the teen pregnancy school. I didn't realize how many pregnant girls were there; I was seriously shocked. I don't know why I was so shocked, but I was. I knew some of the girls because we had gone to school together. It was cool; I was just ready to get this pregnancy over with.

Okay, let me push forward to the week before I had my baby. I walked around the corner because my cousin was fighting with some females. While my fat, pregnant self stood and watched what was going on, a chick that was into it with my cousin came for me. She called me to the street. She wanted to fight me, even though it was obvious I was nine months pregnant. Y'all, I was as big as ever.

Apparently, old girl thought because I was pregnant, I wasn't going to come to the street. But guess what? I went there, with my big pregnant self! On my way to the street, I grabbed a bat out of a little boy's hands and went straight to swinging it. Ole girl had me all messed up, for real.

Some city employees who were working on the street came and tried to break it up. They grabbed me, saying, "Baby girl, you don't need to be fighting. You might hurt your baby, or you may go into labor." I was not trying to hear it. I was on 10, and at that point, I had tunnel vision, seeing only that target.

During those moments, I had forgotten I was even pregnant. I was going nuts, for real. I totally lost it. Oh, but oh, when ole girl saw I was trying to knock her head off with that bat, she started running. The chick was hollering, telling people, "Get her, she's crazy."

Oh, I'm crazy now, huh? Wow! I'm thinking, 'You started it and I'm going to finish it.' I felt she tried me because I was pregnant. I had nothing to do with the altercation. When I say nothing, I mean nothing. I was just watching, because I knew my cousin had hands and I wasn't worried about her losing the fight. The city workers finally got me somewhat calmed down and someone went and got my mama and daddy. They came around the corner and made me go home. Mama was fussing at me the whole way.

I promise y'all, I was tuning her out. Anybody who knew me knew it would take me anywhere from three to four hours to completely calm down. All I could think about was how after I had my baby, I was going to beat the mess out of ole girl who tried me while I was pregnant.

Chapter 3 – The Delivery

I woke up that morning and something felt different. I wasn't sure what was going on with me. I got up, showered, got dressed, and ate some cereal. Then I felt it - a sharp pain in my back. It didn't feel like that would be the day my baby would come. I didn't know if I was having a boy or a girl. This was before they had the technology to tell you the sex of the baby. I wanted a girl. I had all brothers, so I was "team girl." I was watching TV and the pain shifted to the bottom of my stomach. The contractions were coming and going. At that point, I could take the pain. This went on for two hours, and then the pains started to get closer together. I decided to tell my mama.

By then, the contractions were about five minutes apart. My daddy told me to get ready to go to the hospital. I was so scared. The pain was horrible. So then, my mama rushed me to the hospital. We got there and they prepped me. They checked me, and guess what? I was only two centimeters dilated; I had eight centimeters to go. I was put in a room, and while having contractions, I played hangman and SOS with my cousin. When the contractions got closer to two minutes apart, I was ready to cuss. But my mama was there so, that wasn't happening.

That baby needed to exit, stage left, or right. I wanted it out of me! I was over it; trust me. A girl in the room next to me was hollering, and that made me mad. So, I started hollering at her. But I tell you, I found out real fast why she was hollering. The staff exams were very painful.

Here came the doctor, talking about, "I have to check you."

I was like "no," but I knew it had to be done. Four hours in, he checked me, and I was at seven and a half centimeters. It was getting close.

The nurse came to check my blood pressure and pain hit. I grabbed her hair and pulled her to my chest.

She said, "Please let go of my hair."

I'm like, 'Not until this pain goes away.' When I let her hair go, she went and got one of those blue hospital hats to put on her head to make sure I couldn't grab her hair again. I did apologize for it y'all.

The doctor came in two hours later because I said it felt like I had to have a bowel movement. He checked me and I was at eight centimeters. He broke my water. Stuff got real then. This child was on its way. I immediately went from eight to ten centimeters. I pushed, and the nurse told me to pant. You see, back in 1979, they took you to the delivery room to give birth.

They got me to the delivery room, put me on the table, put my legs in the stirrups, and then it was time to push. I was really scared, but wanted this baby, who was hurting me so badly, to be out of me. The doctor had to cut me, and once that happened, the head came out. I pushed, and the shoulders came out. Then the rest of the baby came out. They flipped the baby over and said, "It's a girl."

I was so freaking happy, y'all. I was now officially the mother of a baby girl. Just what I wanted. A mother at 16, still a baby myself...wow!

Chapter 4 - Teen Mom Life

I remember the day I went home with my baby girl. She weighed 7lbs, 7oz. She was 21 inches long with a head full of hair and I was her mama. A 16-year-old mama. Whew, I promise y'all, I had no idea what I was doing. I got up that morning excited, and somewhat scared about going home. There would not be any nurses to help me with her, and no nursery to send her to when I wanted to sleep. Oh well, it was a part of being a mom, a teen mom at that.

Then it was me and my baby girl against the world. I vowed to myself I would be the best mom I could be. Now, mind you, I was only 16 years old - still young and wanting to have fun. I got my baby and myself dressed, and my mama and daddy came to pick us up. My mama asked me did I call my baby daddy and tell him I had her.

I told her, "Yes, but he wasn't home, and when I finally talked to him, he was mad because I didn't give her his last name."

Now back then, if you weren't married, the baby had to have the mother's last name, which I tried to explain to him. He asked me when I was going home, but I didn't tell him because I was mad at him.

Fast forward...I got home and got myself and A'Lya settled in. My boobs were hurting so badly, and they had tripled in size. It was just crazy. I tried to breastfeed, but it hurt so bad, I couldn't. I had to suffer until the milk dried up.

Chapter 5 - Unexpected Visitor

I was in the bathroom and suddenly someone banged on the bathroom door.

I screamed angrily, "Who is it?"

I heard my baby daddy's voice "Open the door. I've been shot."

Okay y'all, I was like, 'What the heck?" I opened the door and he fell into the doorway.

I asked, "Are you okay?"

He said, "I will be." Then he went on to say, "I was on my way to see my daughter, and someone shot me in the back."

When I say this day started off so messed up, I wasn't kidding. I couldn't believe it. I asked, "Why would someone want to shoot you? What did you do?"

My mama called the police and the ambulance. While we were waiting, he wanted to see A'Lya. I brought her to him, and he smiled, and said, "She looks just like me."

I instantly got an attitude and told him, "No, she doesn't. She looks like me, her mama."

He just laughed, even though he was in pain.

The police and ambulance arrived, checked him out and got his information. Thank God it wasn't serious. They dressed the wound and took him to the hospital.

Chapter 6 - Tired, Tired

I was so tired. A'Lya kept me up all night. She slept all day and stayed up all night long. I didn't know I should be sleeping when she slept. Motherhood was kicking my butt, literally. I never thought being a teen mom would be so draining. My life had drastically changed y'all. I could no longer go and kick it with my friends. My daughter was now the center of my life.

When A'Lya was about six months old, I met a guy. He was chocolate, handsome and knew all the right things to say to a young lady. He came right in, taking care of my baby girl, and he swept me off my feet. I fell for him hook, line, and sinker.

He was five years older than me. He knew what to do and say. I looked at it as he was just being a man. Before I knew it, I ended up getting pregnant again, and my baby girl, A'Lya, wasn't even a year old yet. There I went again, round two of being a pregnant teen. I went back to the school for pregnant teenagers, along with a couple of other friends that were there with me the previous year

Fast forwarding...I went out with my baby daddy one night. I got home, showered, and A'Lya and I went to bed about 4 a.m. I woke up thinking I had peed on myself. I sat up and thought, 'Wow, I'm too old to be peeing in the bed.' I got up and checked on A'Lya and went to use the bathroom. The water kept coming out. Now, mind you, my water didn't break with A'Lya, so I didn't know what the heck was going on.

I went and knocked on my mama's door and told her I thought my water had just broken. She jumped up and told me to sit down. I sat down. Then she told me to get up and get dressed so she could take me to the hospital. While I was getting dressed, the pains started. I wasn't due until August, on my birthday, and it was July. I was really scared. My mama woke my brothers up so they could watch A'Lya for me while she took me to the hospital. My daddy was at work. He worked nights, so my mama called him to let him know what was going on.

We got in the car and the labor pains were about five minutes apart. Oh, let me back up. I called Dion, the baby's father, to let him know I was on my way to the hospital. My mama was speeding, and we got stopped by the police. The officer came to the car and my mama told him I was in labor, and my water had broken. He said, "Ma'am, just follow me," and she did.

We arrived at the hospital and Dion was standing outside with a wheelchair. I got out of the car, and he took me up to the sixth floor. They put me in the triage room to check and see if my water had broken. Then they prepped me and took me to the labor room. My mama and Dion were in the labor room with me.

By that time, the labor pains were severe and coming every two minutes. He was by my side trying to comfort me and I was scratching him up. Why not? Heck, if I was in pain, he should be in pain too, right? I was dilating quicky, 2, 4, 6, 8, then 10 centimeters. I got all hooked up at 5 a.m. and had my daughter at 5:45 a.m.

She was not playing. She was ready to come. She weighed 5 lbs. 7 oz., was 20 1/2 inches long, and she came out looking like a Chinese with lots of straight, black hair laying all over her head. I was a mama at age 17, after having A'Lya at age 16. Double trouble. I thought to myself, 'What am I going to do now?'

Chapter 7 - Marriage

Dion asked me to marry him. Let me remind you, I was 17 and couldn't legally get married without one of my parent's permission. My mama was totally against it, but my daddy was okay with it. So, he signed the papers, and I got married to Dion in my parents' living room with a few family and friends - not knowing it was a big mistake. So, there I was, 17 years old and married.

We got a place, and then I had to be a grown woman for sure. I was taking care of two kids, a husband, and a house. Washing clothes, cleaning house, mopping floors, washing the dishes, cooking breakfast, lunch, and dinner. I really didn't know how to cook. It was trial and error. I remember our first argument, I had cooked greens and I didn't season them right. My husband got mad and started telling me that that's not how his mama cooked greens. He said some very hurtful things to me, and I lashed out at him and said some things that I knew would hit below the belt, if you get my drift. Yeah, I had a bad mouth with no filter, and I could be mean as hell! He couldn't take what I was saying to him, so he took his plate of food and threw it in my face while I was holding our baby. You know it was on after that, right?

I sat the baby on the corner of the couch and told her then 2-year-old sister to sit by her to make sure she didn't move. I got up and hit him in his face, and the fight was on. I told him if he ever did that again, I would beat the mess out of him. He pushed me and tried to hit me, but I had gotten to the drawer where I kept the knives. I got a butcher knife out and told him if he came any closer, I would cut him long, wide, and deep! He knew I was not playing, so he left. That was the best thing for him to do. I took my babies and got them ready for bed.

When they were asleep, I cleaned up the mess Dion had made. Dion called me and apologized, but I wasn't trying to hear it. I didn't want him back in the house, and I told him if he came home, his cover and pillow were on the couch waiting on him. I had nothing to say to him.

I told him, "I'm not your mama and if you want her cooking then, you need to take your butt over her house and let her cook for you." I was over it.

When he came home, I was in the bed pretending to be asleep, until he tried to lay down next to me. Oh, heck baby, I told him that his cover and pillow were on the couch and that's exactly where he needed to reside. He tried his best to talk me into letting him sleep in the bed, but that was not happening. No sir, you said too much and did too much so take your good talking self and have a good night on the couch. See ya! I turned over and went to sleep all over the bed and slept well.

I was so frustrated over that fight that I didn't want to try and work things out. He said too much. Once you speak hurtful words, you can't take them back. They are out there, and they keep playing over and over in your head. Dang, could I ever get over this?

Chapter 8 - Fights, More Babies & Cheating

We got past our first fight only to make up, and guess what? I ended up pregnant with my third child. Stairsteps y'all. He wanted me to get an abortion, but I wasn't having it. The arguments got more intense, and he started staying out 'til the wee hours of the morning.

One of his partners told me he was messing around with some chick. I didn't want to believe the guy because he was trying to talk to me, and I figured he was telling me this so I could mess around with him to get back at Dion. It didn't work though. I really didn't think Dion would do that to me. But oh, was I wrong. Things started happening that made it very clear he was cheating. This girl, and her brothers and sisters showed up at my house on some B.S.

I was pregnant, but didn't care, because I was on 10 and ready to fight. He was down at the door pushing me back. I got even madder and ran upstairs to get my gun. On the way down the steps, my brother-in-law grabbed me, picked me up, took me into the living room, and snatched the gun out of my hand. They left and I went off, 'cause how the heck did they know where we lived? What Dion's partner had told me was true. While I was at my mama's house, this man was bringing that girl to our house and sleeping with her in our bed. This explained why he kept forgetting to get my key made.

So, one night I was at my mama's, it was getting late. I was paging him, and he never called me back. I had my mama take me home. We pulled up, and his car was outside. I knocked on the door and there was no answer. Instead of leaving, I walked around the back. On my way, I picked up this big rock and I called myself going to throw it through the sliding glass doors. But instead, because it was so heavy, when I tried to throw it, I threw both the rock and myself through the sliding glass door. At this time, I was more than seven months pregnant with my third child. Once inside, I went straight to the knife drawer, grabbed the butcher knife, and started looking around the house to make sure that girl wasn't hiding anywhere.

After my search, I went up to one of the bedrooms and he was in the bed, drunk and asleep. The room reeked of liquor. After looking in the closet, under the bed, in the girl's bedroom, and a bathroom, I tapped him with the knife and shook him. He woke up to a knife in his face. Looking stunned, he sat up and asked me how I got in. I told him I broke the sliding glass door. He asked me why I did that.

I told him, "To catch your trifling butt cheating."

He wiped his face, sat up on the side of the bed and said, "Ain't nobody in here but me."

I said, "I know because I looked all around before waking you up. But if it had been someone in here, y'all wasn't going to make it out of here. Not the way y'all come in here. You can take that however you like."

He got up to go look at the door. I went to wrap up my hand. My mama kept my kids that night. It was me and him at home. He slept on the floor in front of the door until the office opened so they could fix the glass door. He had the nerve to ask me what he should tell them happened to the glass.

I said, "Tell them the truth. You're a cheater and you been having your side piece in our house when I'm not here and failed to get my key made so I broke the window to catch you with her."

He was like...There you go.

A couple of weeks after that, I got a call from Dion's sister, and she told me that the girl he had been messing around with had birthed a baby and was in the hospital. This girl was claiming that the baby was Dion's.

I was like, "Really, so who is it?" I was so pissed.

She told me the girl's name and what hospital she was in. So, the next morning, I called the hospital and asked for this chick's room and phone number, but they said she was no longer there; she had gone home the previous day... Now y'all know I couldn't wait 'til Dion got his trifling butt home from work. I had packed up his stuff.

He came in all happy-go-lucky, and I was sitting on the couch, pissed. He tried to kiss me, and I pulled away and told him to go and kiss his new baby.

He looked all surprised and asked, "What are you talking about?"

I lost it. I said, "Stop freaking playing with me, dude. You know exactly what I'm talking about. You got a baby with old girl. Did you not know I would find out?"

Now that was the ultimate betrayal. Not just cheating, but getting another woman pregnant? I wanted to kill him. You know a man's favorite line when they get caught is 'it ain't mine.' How the heck do you know it ain't yours if you been sexing her?

I told myself, "OK Shay, keep it clean. Calm down. Breathe in, breathe out."

I told him I wanted him out of there. I said, "Either you leave, or I'll leave." He told me he'd just sleep on the couch.

I said, "Heck no. I don't want to see you at all. I want to kill you for real. Go and stay with that witch you've been seeing and having sex and a baby with. Oh, you can't huh, because she lives with her parents. Not my problem now, is it? You go stay with your mama and daddy before your mama be wearing that black dress!"

He said, "Are you threatening me?"

I told him it wasn't a threat it was a promise. At that point, I couldn't stand him. When he was at work, I was happy. But as soon as I heard his key in the lock, I got an attitude. Having sex was out of the question, and if we did, I made him wear a condom.

I didn't trust him at all. When I did give in after I had our third baby girl, I felt like Ceely in 'The Color Purple'. It felt like he was doing his business on me, no pleasure at all, as I would lay there lifeless, frowning and my skin crawling because I hated him. But I felt I needed to stay with him so my daughters could be raised with both parents. Fights, arguments, and the cheating kept happening, and two more babies. Two more baby girls came ten months apart.

Chapter 9 - Separation

Living life was taking a toll on me. I didn't understand what I had done to deserve any of this. I felt like a fool in that loveless marriage with five daughters, trying to endure and stay for them because I felt like they needed both of us. The arguments and fights had gotten worse. I kept it from my daddy and brothers because I knew if they found out there would be major problems. Besides, I didn't want to tell them until I was sure that I was through with Dion and wasn't ever going back to him.

One day, when Dion left for work, I took the girls and moved in with my parents. I was done. Over it. Over him. I had fought my last fight. I didn't want my daughters to think this was how a man is supposed to treat a woman.

My 5-year-old daughter had come to me one day and said to me, "Mama, why don't you leave daddy?"

I asked her why she would ask that. She said because all y'all do is fight and you're not happy. Out of the mouths of babes. Well, she was right. That's when I knew it was time to leave. I knew he was going to be pissed when he got home, but I didn't care. Oh well, he should have taken his marriage seriously and stopped being a 'ho'

He kept calling me and saying, "You should have left when I didn't care."

Wait...what?? When did you care? Man, please. When did you ever care? I guess your cheating was a sign that you cared, huh? Yeah, right. Miss me with that. He threatened me repeatedly, saying he was going to kill me. He told me he had a bullet with my name on it. Now mind you, he would get so mad at me when I'd be shooting in my daddy's gun range in his basement. He knew I could shoot, and he knew I wasn't scared of him. I told him, "You got to bring butt, to get butt." So, you see, I was bruised but not broken.

The house I had moved out of was my house. My name was on the lease, not his. So, I told him he had to move out, and I had the lights turned off. At first, he refused, but I told him I would let the landlord know he was there, so he went on and moved out. I had the locks changed and got an order of protection to cover me if he tried something. Then the girls and I moved back in. I filed for a divorce, and he would not sign the papers. So, the attorney put it in the newspaper for three months and after that, no reply. I was given a court date. I went to court and the judge granted my divorce and gave me my maiden name back. Yay! I was so happy that I threw myself a divorce party.

We kicked it too. Shoot, I was still young, and I hadn't had much of teenage life because I was married and had kids. It was my time to kick it. So, that's exactly what I did. I started going out and meeting new people. I was working two jobs and still partying, and most of all, taking care of my babies. I was enjoying the single life. Oooowee! I was 5'3", 125 pounds, had long black hair, and dressed nice. You couldn't tell me anything. I had the worse attitude ever. I was mean as heck. I wanted all men to pay for what Dion did to me. I was out for revenge. Hey, I was young and angry, bruised, bent, and hurt and the pain was intense.

Chapter 10 - Pimping

I was the chick that had a champagne appetite with a Kool-Aid pocketbook. I wanted to always have a nice house, car, etc., right? Well, those two jobs weren't getting it. I was dating this dude that hustled in his spare time that put me on. Yep, I was selling lightweight drugs, nothing too much. Then I stopped selling drugs because I started feeling bad, so I started pimping women. I felt justified because it wasn't our sisters. In reality, it was still wrong. At least I treated them right. I didn't have them out walking the streets. I'd set them up with men and take them to the men and the men would have to pay me before any action took place. No exceptions!

I kept them dressed and took care of them. I didn't do them dirty. It paid well and it kept my bills paid. I dressed my daughters nicely and we lived in a nice crib. I also drove a nice car, so we were good. One day one of my girls, Kathy, came to me and said she didn't want to continue to live that life. She said she wanted to settle down, have kids, get married, and get a real job. She said the others felt the same way. So, we sat down and talked about it.

Now, I wasn't doing bad with the two jobs I had. I made decent money. I could take care of my bill and kids. Being the person I was, I let them go because for real, I felt bad, and I'd be damned if someone did my girls that way. I ended up moving into a bigger, nicer home and started doing daycare. Wait, let me back up. I met this guy named RJ. He had pretty eyes and all. He came in helping me. We got married and that's when things turned.

Chapter 11 - Hell Breaks Loose

Now, this man was different. He was very charming and took care of the home. We ended up getting the house he grew up in after we got married. We fixed it up and it was really nice. I got into God's word because I wanted to change my life. I had always felt like I had a calling on my life, but I didn't think God would use me because of the things I had done in my past. My relationship with RJ started out good, but then drugs and cheating came into play. There I went again!

I worked but didn't have to cash my paychecks right away since RJ kept me with money and he took care of my girls. He brought them things he said that no other man could impress them with because they already had it. I got new furniture every year. He spoiled us. But everything that glitters ain't gold. He started gambling and messing up money. He was using drugs. So, needless to say, that started arguments. Oh yeah, he was also cheating.

I guess I was never going to have a man that didn't cheat. Good lawd! I started going to a church in Kansas and got deeply involved. So, he started going to church with us. Now, to the people at church, we looked like a happy couple. What they didn't know was on the way to church we were arguing. But, when we got to the church, the arguing stopped, and we were once again a happy couple who knew how to pretend well. That went on until I just couldn't take it anymore.

Early one morning I got in my car and drove to where he was. The Lord led me there. He had moved out and was staying with this big chick named Thelma, who was obsessed with knowing how I looked and hurting me. Heck, she told me that RJ wanted her to plot how to kill me. Okay, so RJ had her rent him a car. What she didn't know was he wanted that car so he could take these two chicks he was messing with out of town. She found out somehow and reported the car stolen. She also discovered that RJ had cleaned out her bank account. She had gotten my number off RJ's cell phone before he left, and she had the nerve to call me.

She told me her name was Thelma Johnson. I asked her what she wanted, and she said she was calling to talk to me woman to woman. She began to tell me about what RJ had done, how he cleared out her bank account and how he took those girls out of town and wouldn't return the rental car. She was crying and I tried to find some sympathy for her, but I just couldn't.

I told her it was her karma for messing with a married man. She said she didn't know he was married, but when I told her I knew she was lying and threatened to hang up on her, she told the truth. She knew. She said RJ had told her we were having problems and that he had caught me cheating. I laughed so hard. All lies. He's the one who is a cheater, not me. Thelma said she had asked RJ multiple times to see a picture of me and he said no. He said I wasn't cute, and she didn't need to see me. I laughed again. She told me that one day when he went to work, she went into her garage and went through his boxes, where she found our wedding book. She said she looked through it and I was a beautiful bride, and our wedding was pretty.

"I don't know why he lied and told me you weren't cute," she said.

I told her it didn't matter. She shared that he had said a lot of horrible things about me. I told her, "I'm sure he did but, what does that have to do with me? I couldn't care less. He's your problem now and not mine."

She went on to say, "I asked him if he's divorcing you and he said you won't give him a divorce."

I interrupted her and told her he was lying. The truth was, I had filed for a divorce, and he wouldn't sign the papers. I asked her to tell RJ to sign the papers so we could be done legally.

She said, "We're supposed to get married."

"Congratulations" I said, sarcastically.

"Well, I don't know about that now after what he's done," she mumbled.

I told her, "Y'all can work it out. Chile please, keep him over there. I don't want him."

Then I told her I had to hang up because it was time for me to go to work. I wished her a good day and told her I hoped things worked out between her and RJ.

Now y'all know I had to call my sister and tell her this mess. My sister was like, "What the heck is she crying to you for? Not your problem at all. She made her bed now she must lie in it. I don't feel sorry for her...old witch."

I just laughed.

Chapter 12 - Life Change

After all the hell I'd been through, all the heartaches and bumps and bruises, I needed to get right with the Lord, ask Him to forgive me, and begin to live right. After all, God had kept me three times from being killed by men that either I had been in a relationship with or one who shot at me when he tried to talk to me, and I wouldn't talk to him.

God had 'sho nuff' kept me. He kept my mind when I should've gone crazy. He kept me. I knew that I could've been locked up and in jail for always fighting. I should have been in prison, but God. Yes, He kept me.

I was tore up from the floor up. I needed a check-up from the neck up. Those times when I could have been shot up and wasn't, I thought it was because I was so tough. I hadn't realized that it was God's grace and mercy that kept me. I didn't realize it was because He had a plan for my life. Glory!

I went to church one Sunday morning and the Bishop was preaching. His title was "I should have been dead and gone but, Lord, you let me live on," or something to that effect. I promise y'all I thought he was telling the congregation all of my business. He was preaching to me. It was like no one else was there. It was directed towards me.

Now, that wasn't the case at all. He was just preaching the sermon that God had put on his heart. The sermon that would change my life. The sermon that God orchestrated for me to hear because He knew even though I was mean and even evil at times, I had a heart of gold and that I needed to be healed from my past and delivered so that He could mold me into the woman of God He wanted me to be.

Chapter 13 - Pain in the Process

I enrolled in Faith Bible College. I took three different classes. One of the classes was on deliverance. One of the other classes was Living a Christian Life According to God's Way. I cannot think of the name of the third one, but it taught me how to put a sermon together. I thought becoming a Christian was going to be a walk in the park and that my troubles were going to be over. Oh, but was I wrong. The devil and his imps got busier than ever, sending one distraction after the other.

I met this guy. He was a tall drink of water...ooooweee. He was good looking. He treated me like a queen, cooked candlelight dinners, attended church with me. He didn't fuss, smoke, or drink other than an occasional glass of wine that we both drank at dinner. Our relationship got intimate. I felt in my heart he was the one. During the next eight to ten years, we were on-again, off-again, keeping a friendship through Facebook. He was the only man that I ever really loved. We got back together in 2018, only to break up because of me not being able to go or do like he wanted. Then we got back together through a text message in 2019. Jay said he let me go to see if I would come back. That's when I found out who he really was.

Our relationship was good. We hung out sometimes, me, him, and my grands. They were crazy about Jay. I loved Jay. Then I realized Jay hadn't been honest with me in the beginning. Oh, I was still in church and preaching, for those of you who may have thought I had backslid.

Jay cussed like a sailor, and he drank occasionally. But, he smoked, as my daddy would call it, that wacky tobacky. That was him, and one day, we were talking, and he told me that he was different in the beginning because he didn't want me to walk away if I knew the real Jay. Our whole relationship was based on a lie. Wow! But I loved him. I dealt with it until his bestie started her shenanigans. At first, I didn't say anything about it, and she really got loose. I spoke up and Jay got mad. Really? By now I had put two and two together.

He used to mess with her, and it was evident she had a problem with me. But that's neither here nor there. He got sick and I was there for him. However, I felt as if nothing I did was ever good enough. I found out on Facebook that we had gotten engaged. Yep, that's how I found out. He asked me if I had I seen what he put on Facebook, and I said no. I went on Facebook and there it was. We had gotten engaged on October 28, 2019. Very romantic proposal, huh? He then started to treat me badly. He was mean to me, and for what? His mouth was off the chain, the disrespect from his bestie, and ohhhh honey, I was not having it. The things she would insinuate. She was letting me know things were being said about me without coming right out and telling me. Don't get me wrong, Jay was a good man. He just wasn't a good man for me, and I knew it. I had known it for a while, but I loved him and wanted to be there for him.

The reality was, he wanted or acted like he wanted the bestie. So, we broke up. This time, for good. You see, when a woman (me) leaves a man for herself so she can find herself, she (me) won't return. He blocked me on Facebook and Messenger and said he blocked his bestie as well. Come to find out, she's unblocked, and they are hanging out 'til the wee hours of the morning. Happy for y'all.

Okay, here's the deal. We weren't good for each other because we were unequally yoked. I didn't do the things he did, so there was an issue in our relationship. Then there was the bestie, the other issue in our relationship.

    I will always love Jay and his girls. I wish him the best in life, and I pray he's found happiness. He deserves it. This heartbreak hit differently than the others y'all. I played it in my mind that it didn't hurt me, and I was not bothered. In reality, I was deeply hurt. What made it hurt even more was knowing he didn't care how I felt. I had to pull myself out of that rut, realizing that 'this too shall pass' and that God wanted me to focus on me, and on my relationship with Him.

Chapter 14 - After the Pain

Finally, I'm over the hurt. Do I think about him sometimes? Well, of course. I pray for him and his daughters daily. I even have a prayer written down for them, posted on the wall in my prayer closet. After all, we had good times, and I cherish those memories. After the pain, I really got back to business. Then along came this pandemic, COVID-19, and shut down the city. We're all quarantined. Locked down. It's the perfect time to develop a better relationship with God, study more, pray more, do a self-evaluation, and get cleansed of all the junk that has had me bound. In this time of lockdown, I've gotten deeper into my Word. I've started a vision board, got a desk in my room and I even started writing my gospel stage plays again. I'm motivated now.

God has given me more plays to write. Life-changing plays. I'm about my Father's business now. Pain changes you. If you don't allow it to break you, it will make you. I've learned that you should never compromise your walk with God. Do not allow the devil and his imps to get you off the course where God has placed you. The devil is conniving, and he will send the very things he knows you like to distract you, to get you off course, so he can kill, steal, and destroy your destiny.

That's why you must stay focused and prayed up! Because after the pain, there will be joy. God will elevate you through the painful process, and, honey, you will most definitely know it was Him, because it will be clear you couldn't have done it on your own. God's plan for your life is the best. Allow Him to write the next chapters of your life! It may feel like the end, but it is truly the beginning. I pray that my life story has helped you in some way. My story is much deeper, and I have so much more to share, but I'll save the rest for another time, another book.

Chapter 15 - After the Pain, You Can Start Over

Some people grow through failed relationships, others never recover.

They speak only of the past because they can't get beyond it. What's the answer? You need to see your past mistakes, hurts, and even failures as steppingstones rather than stumbling blocks! How do you do that? I'm so glad you asked. You do it by starting with the following three steps...

1) You must PROCESS. You've got to PROCESS emotions, such as regret. When it comes to emotions, the only way out is THROUGH.
2) You must DECIDE. Don't look at yourself as being down. Change your mindset to think that you're either up or you're getting up. Don't accept defeat. Get up and try again
3) You must REMEMBER. The moment you accept God's forgiveness, you no longer have a past. You only have a FUTURE. You're free to get on with your life.

Pain, heartbreak, disappointment, and failure are steppingstones to your FUTURE. If you fail at some things, just know that it's not the end of the road for you. You get up, dust yourself off, and begin a new journey. God forgives and forgets. Keep your hand in God's hand and trust Him to lead you down the path to your bright future. Consider yourself as the "Up and Coming Attraction." You see, **After the Pain**, you are well on your way to your destiny.

Be blessed in the Mighty Name of Jesus Christ!

More Pain – A Shattered Heart

In 2010, I lost my daddy, the very first man I ever loved! It was an unbearable pain. October 30, 2010 is a day I will never forget. It's the day that my world fell apart and the day that my heart shattered into a million pieces.

In May of 2015, my auntie Alvena Henderson was called home to take her rest after a lifetime of singing for the Lord and preaching His Word. Again, my heart was shattered.

In 2016 my mama went home to be with the Lord. January 11, 2016, an unforgettable day, one I can never erase from my mind. It was devastating to watch her take her last breath and wave goodbye. Once again, my heart was shattered.

In 2018, my sister took her last breath and went to sit at the feet of Jesus. She served Him with her whole heart. My heart hadn't had time to mend from the previous losses. There were, shattered pieces of my heart everywhere.

In April of 2019 on the 9th day, God called my brother's name and took him home. I knew that he was no longer suffering, he had a brand-new heart, and was able to walk around heaven all day. But I was still struggling with the loss of my sister, and it was almost more than my heart could take.

Losing loved ones is never easy. I've lost both sets of grandparents, uncles on both sides, aunties, cousins, friends, play sons and play daughters, the pain is intense. The tears fall with each memory of them all. The memories bring back a smile. Their wings were ready, but my heart wasn't.

"That Smile"

So you tried to hide behind that smile,
that spoke volumes, even though
I still couldn't see what was right there in front of me
That smile that lied with each upward bend
in each corner of your mouth.

That smile I got lost in
That smile I thought was from within
That smile that told the real story
But my eyes were disillusioned
to what that smile really meant
So was you trying to hide behind that sexy innocent smile
While baiting me into a web of deceit and betrayal

That smile, that has hidden agendas and
distrust written all over it
That misleading smile, that convinces, while yet lying
Yeah, that smile, that smiles at you,
as if it is telling the truth, the whole truth and
nothing but the truth

Hold up...Hold up
Pause for a sec
While I catch my breath and try to understand
my thoughts of
that smile of yours
that voice
that laughter
that can cast a spell

In reality it's all just a facade,
created to manipulate and shatter
a woman's dreams of finding that one man
who is loyal and real and honest
You know that one man that plays no games and
will tell the truth even if it hurts you

But all the while is very careful not to offend or
cause you any pain
A man who's not into playing games or
hiding behind his smile of deceit
That smile that plays with a heart that longs to love and
be loved again

Who loses in the end is the heart that is pure and
willing to smile back at the smile that she thought was true
I guess you never know what truly lies behind a smile.

Sometimes you have to lose to win again
After being captured by a smile
that was all just make-believe
It takes me back to that song...
"Smiling faces tell lies...They don't tell the truth"

Ha...fool me once, shame on you,
fool me twice, shame on me
Let me tell you, that will never be me again
Hmm...that Smile

"The Side Effects of You"

The side effects of you keep me at a place where I want to stay
but a part of me wants to keep you away.
The side effects of you make me sad and all so blue.
The side effects of you let me know
some men don't mean what they say or say what they mean.

The side effects of you have kept me off course
lonely and frustrated
Man, this stuff is overrated.
The side effects of you have made me give up on love and
pack my heart neatly away upon the corner of my shelf,
high in my closet with a NO TRESPASSING sign
all because men are usually always lying.

The side effects of you have left a huge tear in my heart
a heart that you promised not to break
but instead of giving, you were always taking...

The side effects of you make me not want to trust another,
even though they come from another mother
To me, they are all the same
Liars. Manipulators. Cheaters.
Always playing with a woman's emotions.

The side effects of you...hmm...
make me realize that you're but a coward
awakening my love and having no intentions
of loving me back
You said what you said to get what you wanted.

The side effects of you left me broken hearted
unable to trust because of your lies and betrayal.
The side effects of you taught me that the three words
"I Love You" may very well mean nothing
They're just words spoken without any true meaning.

You gave me enough to keep me with you,
but when I got tired and said you had to go
you left me with mixed emotions
of how this thing called 'Love' is supposed to be

Now that I don't want you,
you won't leave me alone,
proclaiming your undying love for me
Hahahahaha. That's really funny.

You say you always cared,
but you were scared to love me in ways
that you felt you could
Instead, you did you at the expense of me.
The side effects of you left me feeling empty and lost,
my heart all torn apart.

The side effects of you left me reflecting
how I gave you 100% of me and
you chose to only give me 20% of you
WOW, what a big difference.

The side effects of you I was too blind to see,
by your smile, by the words you spoke,
by the way you held me making me feel all safe and loved

only to finally realize that you never loved me,
but you only played a role to get what you got, my heart.
Only to mishandle it and not treat it with tender loving care
but left it all battered and bruised and broken
and now, I'm left with all these side effects of you.

"I Got Lost"

I got lost Oh yes, me
I found myself off kilter and juggling
with my knowledge of right and wrong and wrong and right
Tired of being alone and wanting to be loved and to give love

I got lost in wanting someone to want me
in all the ways that I want to be wanted
Living in this world of make-believe and
afraid to be real with myself
about how I truly feel

I got lost in putting on this facade that
I have it all together and I'm okay with how my life is
while in reality, longing eternally for that special someone to
come and rescue me from the prison that I made for myself
You know, that once upon a time kind of love
My bad, I really mean fairy tale kind of love,
that only happens in the storybooks

I got lost in a stack of to-do-lists
I got to be this woman who can make it do what it do
while maintaining and withstanding
and holding out on her physical needs
and balancing a career and motherhood,
single motherhood at that
Trying to be all that I could be

I got lost in real life,
shielding my heart carefully for NO MORE HURTS,

let downs, and disappointments
or a relationship based on lies,
being torn down only to find myself getting back up

I got lost in tears at night
had no one to hold me tight
so I pressed my way forward
psyched myself out
into believing that I was good being alone and
not allowing anyone into my space
who was I fooling?

I got lost in living this facade for people to see
that I forgot who I was
I made a character out of a storybook
made me a life that if no one else cared about it,
I did, and I found myself content with the skin I was in

I got lost in trying to stay balanced on the balance beam
of the story I wrote for me
often trying to find blame in others and
not myself, realizing that I was truly not happy,
only insisting on this skin that I'm in

I got lost in the thoughts of finally having someone in my life
to say all the things I want to hear...
you know the things that make you feel good inside,
even if it's all a lie

I got lost in your hugs and kisses
all the wishes of a 'us' hanging out talking and
I got lost in your laughter...your smile...

in your looks that kept me mesmerized

I got lost in running away from you
trying to find me a safe zone
So that I wouldn't feel so vulnerable
I got lost in my thoughts of you…
STOP! Danger Zone!

No need to tread because my thoughts are merely my thoughts
If you only knew then you would see my inner chastity
Then where would we be? Watch out now!
I got lost and some days I wondered if I wanted to be found
Or continue to live in this story I made for me
Titled "I GOT LOST!"

"I Heard My Daddy Saying to Me"

Baby girl, I hate I had to leave you...
But it was my time to go...It's really beautiful here...
So, baby girl, you don't have to continue to shed a tear...
I'm here with my mama and my dad and
all of my brothers and sisters too...
So please baby girl, you don't have to be blue...
I know you will miss me as I will miss you too...
Remember that I'm looking down on you...
So I will always be around...
Maybe not in the physical, but forever in the spirit...
It was very hard for me to leave you...
You were my Boo...
I knew it would hurt you...
So I stayed as long as I could...trying to hang in there...
So that you would not be so sad...
The truth is baby girl, I was tired...
Tired of all the pain...The feeding tube...the catheter...
Wanting to eat some real food and drink me some pop...
But was only able to get fed through this tube...
Heck, I couldn't even taste my food in the end...
I was more quiet than I ever been...
Preserving my breath for what I only wanted to say...
The love that I have for you...is simply wonderful...
The moment you were born,
I was the proudest daddy in the world...
God gave me my precious little girl...
At that moment you looked me in my eyes...
I knew you had me wrapped around your little finger...
Hook line and sinker...Oh yes, that's what I was...
My baby girl...My world...I tried not to make a difference...

But, it was really hard not to do...
My life changed the moment your mama had you...
No matter what I was or what people thought I was...
The good or the bad...
when you looked at me you could see no wrong,
that kept me strong...Oh yes, baby girl...
You were most definitely my world, my pride, and joy...
So hold on to all the many, many memories that we shared...
And remember that your daddy always cared...
So it's never goodbye...but, it's only see you later...
because baby girl now I am healthy,
I got new pair of legs and
walking around without any help and taking very long steps...
walking around with all my family and some of my friends...
on streets paved with gold...
oh yeah, remember I'm your pot of gold
at the end of the rainbow...
So continue to do what you have to do...make me proud...
cause just like I boasted and bragged on you on earth...
I'm still doing it here...I'm able to see where you're headed...
even before you see...so baby girl, go get it...
it's out there waiting...see you later...
remember that I'm not gone...
you carry me with you each day
right there in your heart!

"My Fault"

My fault, I didn't follow my first mind, instead,
I drew the line...Stepped out of self...
knowing better but doing the opposite!!
What was I really trying to find...

My fault, for wanting to be loved and settling...
instead of being more selective...
looking through a stained tarnished glass mirror,
seeing a reflection of beauty instead of truth

My fault, yes, once again falling off,
backsliding, treading water,
doing me, not doing me, wanting love,
not wanting to be loved,
afraid of love, afraid of letting go fully,
not giving enough, or maybe giving too much!

Wait!!!! Hold up a minute...Cut...
What the heck is wrong with me?

Oh yeah, it's my fault that I can't get it together
so that I can make that major decision…
to take off the blinders of reality and face my fears...
so I can grow in all the areas
that I know I need growth in!

No one to blame but self!!
So, check this...
I'm going to take off those shades of 'could ofs'
focus on my first true love...you know that One

who has never forsaken you…
left you even in your darkest hours...
the One I ran away from instead of running to
all because I wanted to do me!

The One who has always loved me
regardless of the things I've done...
the One who looks beyond my faults and sees my needs...
the One who is forgiving and even forgets
when others hold your past and e
ven your present over your head...
the One first real and true love of my life...

I find myself running...back to Him,
where it's safe and I can be who He has called me to be!
So you see, my faults are no longer because
God has forgiven them!!!
Now, I move carefully and more wisely towards my destiny
that He has for me!
Oh yeah, my fault, I thought you knew…
my first true love is God!

About the Author

Sharon Ewell is the mother of six daughters and has 26 grandchildren and two great grandsons. She is a gospel play writer and business owner of "Sha' Cakes the World of Swirls."

Sharon's mission is to help women to avoid going down the road she took by letting them know that with God as the main ingredient, they can get past the pain of their past.

Sharon is a minister of the Gospel of Jesus Christ. She attended Faith Bible College and obtained certificates in Faith Living and Deliverance.

Sharon's first book "After the Pain – You Can Start Again" is based on her life's disappointments, her struggles through the pain of her past, and how she overcame those obstacles.

www.ingramcontent.com/pod-product-compliance
Lightning Source LLC
Chambersburg PA
CBHW072039080526
44578CB00007B/536